30 Minutes

... To Write a Report

Patrick Forsyth

KOGAN PAGE

First Indian Edition 2003
Reprinted 2008

Kogan Page India Private Limited
4737/23 Ansari Road,
Daryaganj
New Delhi 110 002

ISBN-10: 81-7554-074-5
ISBN-13: 978-81-7554-074-3

Published by Vinod Vasishtha for Kogan Page India Private Limited, 4737/23 Ansari Road, Daryaganj, New Delhi - 110 002.

Printed and bound at Print Perfect, New Delhi - 110 064.

CONTENTS

The 30 Minutes Series

The Kogan Page 30 Minutes Series has been devised to give your confidence a boost when faced with tackling a new skill or challenge for the first time.

So the next time you're thrown in at the deep end and want to bring your skills up to scratch or pep up your career prospects, turn to the *30 Minutes Series* for help!

Titles available are:
30 Minutes Before A Meeting
30 Minutes Before A Presentation
30 Minutes to Boost Your Communication Skills
30 Minutes to Boost Your Self Esteem
30 Minutes to Brainstorm Great Ideas
30 Minutes to Deal With Difficult People
30 Minutes to Get Your Own Way
30 Minutes to Get Promoted
30 Minutes to Improve Your Networking Skills
30 Minutes to Make the Right Decision
30 Minutes to Manage Your Time Better
30 Minutes to Market Yourself
30 Minutes to Master the Internet
30 Minutes to Motivate Your Staff
30 Minutes to Negotiate a Better Deal
30 Minutes to Plan a Project
30 Minutes to Solve that Problem
30 Minutes to Succeed in Business Writing
30 Minutes to Write a Business Plan
30 Minutes to Write a Marketing Plan
30 Minutes to Write a Report
30 Minutes to Write Sales Letters

Available from all good bookseller.
For further information on the series, please contact:

INTRODUCTION

> 'Writing is easy, all you do is sit staring at a blank sheet of paper until the drops of blood form on your forehead.'
>
> Gene Fowler

Writing, especially business writing, often seems a real chore. And reports are, by definition, among the longer forms of business writing. But reports have an important role to play, so they have to be written and written well. If your first feeling when a report writing job drops on your desk is one of apprehension or even dread, then this book is for you. It will help too, even if you have written many reports, but want to improve your writing skills just a little.

Report writing might be called a career skill. In other words, there are many jobs where the ability to execute it well is a prerequisite for success and even for career progress. If you present a well-thought out document, people are more likely to want to read what you put in front of them, and to take notice of what it says. This is true of certain other skills, and, in common with them, writing a good report does not just happen; study – and practice, of course – can make it much easier.

The series is designed to achieve its aims promptly in a minimal space. So, without further ado, we will get into the 'how to' of report writing.

Patrick Forsyth
Touchstone Training & Consultancy
17 Clocktower Mews
London N1 7BB
Spring 1997

1

THE OPPORTUNITY

'It is the business equivalent of an open goal.' This description was applied to presentations (by a character in Video Arts' excellent training film *I wasn't prepared for that*), but it is equally applicable to reports. It may seem odd to suggest that every report you write represents an opportunity, but the word does not overstate the case and it deserves its place in this first chapter heading.

Prevailing standards

When did you last have to read a report written by someone else? Did you enjoy doing so, or at least find it easy? What sort of impression did it leave of its topic and its writer? Did it prompt you to agree with its message or make you spring into action? Perhaps not. Too often reports are not well written. At best, a bad report causes annoyance; at worst, active hostility.

Why is a good report such a rare comodity. For all sorts of reasons: reports are written in a rush, they are modelled on some outdated format or formula, or they are actually standard documents, perhaps tweaked just a little to meet a new requirement. In addition, they often have faults that almost guarantee that they will be a chore to read. They lack structure, logic or style. They take ten words to say something that could be said in three. Such reports are difficult to understand and may actually misinform, thus failing in their intended purpose.

Whatever the reasons, it matters. Writing is not a skill that we are born with; and the techniques and habits we build up are not things that cannot be changed. Training – courses or just studying a book like this and resolving to try a few new approaches – can certainly make a difference, and do so quickly. I regularly see people going away from courses I run on various aspects of business writing having made radical changes to practices they walked in with. Thinking through the process can really make a difference and new, improved, habits can be established quite quickly.

There is a strong element of habit at work here. Much is written on 'automatic pilot', and practices and style that dilute what could be good business writing continue because we have stopped thinking about exactly what we are trying to do.

The worst case

As with so many things, what creates quality is not one single factor, but a combination of things. If a report is not considered, if it is dashed off in haste, poorly checked and consists of a structureless jumble of jargon, gobbledegook and office-speak, without style or clarity, if its language is ill-chosen and it is overlong; then the net effect will be a disaster.

Figure 1.1 shows an extreme, albeit caricatured, example of the worst kind of business writing; so much so that subtitles are necessary to highlight any real meaning.

The point here is not, in fact, just to criticise prevailing standards in a negative way. But if they do leave something to be desired that clearly provides an opportunity for those who take the trouble to create something better for their readers. What you do can stand out: you can achieve what you want, and create a positive image too. Indeed, the central message of this short book is that it is comparatively easy to ensure that this is always the case.

Easily influenced: for good or ill

Not only does producing a good report need care in various ways, it is a delicate process. In other words, it is all too easy to dilute the precise sense you are aiming at. One sentence, one phrase, even one ill-chosen word can diminish the clarity, the impact, or both. Attention to detail to avoid such faults is, as we shall investigate further, vital.

Of course, the opposite is also true and small differences can enhance a report in many ways. One particularly well-chosen phrase can transform a routine paragraph or section of a report into something striking or memorable. Just look at the 'open goal' of the first sentence in this chapter. That phrase surely has more impact than simply saying 'good report writing can provide opportunities'.

But what makes a good report is not a matter for academic discussion. The final arbiter of what works is, of course, the reader.

Reader expectations

Psychologists are not the only group guilty of introducing a profusion of jargon into business, but one member of

Standard progress report

(for those with no progress to report)

During the survey period which ended on 14 February, considerable progress has been made in the preliminary work directed towards the establishment of the initial activities. (We are getting ready to start, but we have not done anything yet.) The background information has been reviewed and the functional structure of the various component parts of the project have been matched with appropriate human resources. (*We looked at the project and decided George should lead it.*)

Considerable difficulty has been encountered in the selection of optimum approaches and methods, but this problem is being attacked vigorously and we expect the development phase will proceed at a satisfactory rate. (*George is reading the brief.)* In order to prevent the unnecessary duplication of previous work in the same field, it was necessary to establish a project team which has conducted a quite extensive tour through various departments with immediate relevance to the study. *(George and Mary had a nice time visiting everyone.)*

The Steering Committee held its regular meetings and considered important policy matters pertaining to the overall organisational levels of the line and staff responsibilities that devolve on the personnel associated with the specific assignments resulting from the broad functional specifications. *(Which means ...?)* It is believed that the rate of progress will continue to accelerate as necessary personnel become available to play their part in the discussions that must precede decisions. *(We really will do something soon – if we can.)*

Figure 1.1 Gobbledegook: An example from the office notice board. (Reproduced from the author's longer text on this subject, *How to be Better at Writing Reports and Proposals,* Kogan Page.)

that profession did coin a particular phrase that sticks in my memory: *cognitive cost*. An example will serve to make the meaning clear. Imagine wanting to quickly sort out a problem on your computer. Not knowing how to do it, you turn to the manual. For many people a glance at the open book says clearly – shouts, more likely – 'This is going to be difficult'. Such a document is said to have a high cognitive cost: it is densely written, and that it will prove difficult to follow is obvious at a glance.

Reports should aim at precisely the opposite. They should *appear* easy to read at first glance, so a good, accessible style is crucial. Readers are asking themselves questions at this stage: 'Will this be easy? Time consuming? Confusing? Frustrating?' and so on. If, as they begin to read, you can quickly get them saying to themselves that your report *does* look readable, so much to the good.

So what does the report reader really want?

Specific requirements and rewards

Focusing on the reader is central to the whole tenor of this book, and we will return to it. But it is possible to list certain factors of immediate relevance to set the scene. You only have to keep in mind the occasions when you are a reader rather than a writer.

Key factors include making sure what is written is:

- **Brief**; or at least as brief as content and purpose allow (succinct is an appropriate word)
- Clear and **understandable**
- **Precise**, saying exactly what you want (and not including lots of extraneous material)
- In **their language** (at an appropriate level of technicality)

- **Simple**, rather than complex or convoluted
- Set out with a **logical structure**
- Adequately **descriptive**.

Another overriding factor is worth mentioning. Readers need not only to feel that a report is in the right language for them, they appreciate it if there is evidence that their viewpoint has been considered throughout, and the report has been tailored to their needs. For example, you may sometimes need to write two versions of a document, perhaps one for technical people and a non-specialists' version, so that both groups have a feeling of being specially catered for.

As a result, your reports will *seem* readable, indeed they *will be* readable, and your reward is that they will actually be read. Further, and most important of all, there is some chance of the result you want actually occurring. This may mean that people take note, or take action, so you need to know what you want to achieve. Writing reports needs to be seen as a means to end. You need to be clear *why* you are writing and this brings us to the question of setting clear objectives.

Objectives are, logically, part of adequate preparation and that is the subject of the next chapter.

2

PREPARATION AND DRAFTING

It was Peter de Vries who said: 'I love being a writer. What I can't stand is the paperwork.' You may be forgiven for thinking that report writing would be all very well but for the grisly process of deciding the message and getting it down on paper. Sometimes you feel you know what to say, but it is difficult to translate it from mind to paper. At others, it is the initial process of pulling together what to say that forms an earlier hurdle. A systematic approach does help.

This chapter is about deciding what to write and tackling the initial stages promptly and accurately; preparation is the first step to creating a good report. Note that shape and structure are left until Chapter 3, and the details of use of language are dealt with in Chapter 4. The need to dissect the process makes it necessary to take one element at a time, though they overlap in their use and importance.

The first question: why?

No one should ever, repeat ever, put 'pen to paper' without being able to answer the question 'why am I writing it?' and do so in a straightforward, accurate and precise way. Particular purposes aside, there are plenty of general reasons that may make a report necessary. It may be simply to *record* information, but reports are rarely just 'about' something: they are also intended to:

- inform and/or explain
- recommend
- motivate
- prompt or play a part in debate
- persuade
- reinforce (prior discussions/communication)
- instruct

and all these reasons are not, of course, mutually exclusive. You may have several of these intentions (or others still), and you must be clear both about what they are and about their respective priority. For example, the intention to change attitudes may be a longer term aim and one report can only play a part in the ongoing process that aims to achieve it.

Every report needs clear objectives

Objectives specify not what you want to *say*, but what you want to *achieve* by saying it; they are *desired results*. Clarity is important. Your objectives must not be convoluted. They must remain easily in mind (not least as you write) and act *directionally*: that means they must help you to decide the exact length, style, content and so on that will create the right report to do the particular job in hand; and do it effectively.

When thinking about 'why', it may be useful to bear in mind a much-quoted acronym which says any good objectives should be SMART:

- **S**pecific
- **M**easurable
- **A**chievable
- **R**ealistic, and
- **T**imed.

This acronym can also be applied to report writing. A simple example illustrates the principle at work here:

SMART objectives: an example

Imagine you are responsible for some matter of policy within your company. Changes are necessary (perhaps because of a need to save money; the details do not matter). You have to hold a meeting at which you intend that all the heads of section will agree the change, and decide to send them a short report ahead of the meeting. Your objectives for this are as follows:

- To ensure that the group support your recommendations, yet can make an informed decision based on a prior reading of the pros and cons of the case; and
- To prompt the decision to be made without long debate or acrimony.

Both the above are specific. Both are also measurable; simple observation and judgement at and after the meeting will tell you if you have succeeded in your aim.

- You aim to include in the report just the right content to make the above likely; for example, too little explanation and you might have a long discussion on your hands, too much and people might not bother to read it.

Your next thought should aim to make sure your objective is achievable. It must also be realistic.

- Let us assume here that you have picked a topic that is somewhat controversial and therefore not a realistic possibility to agree in one meeting without more elaborate measures.
- Your *timing* here hinges on the meeting; you decide, say, that the report needs to be circulated three weeks before the meeting, and are aiming to have the issue resolved on that day.

The above follows the SMART principles.

Keep your readers in mind

Never forget your readers when setting objectives. Otherwise, writing your report will be like playing darts in the dark. It may even be that separate groups of people, to whom you plan to deliver essentially the same message, need different treatment. Always consider:

- Who the report is for
- Whether they form a homogeneous group (and, if not, what sub-groups are involved)
- The reasons they want or need the report (even if this will have to be explained to them)

- What content they will want included, and in what detail
- What they will not want included.

You also need to look at the results that readers may anticipate from reading the report; eg, they may want to be able to make an informed decision about something.

Clearly, you will benefit from knowing something about your actual or potential readers. The more you know about, for instance, the kind of people they are (young/old, experienced/inexperienced), their level of expertise or knowledge in relation to the topic, their likely attitudes and reactions (will they find it interesting, unimportant, or new to them?), the better. Certainly, whatever you write will be better received if it is well directed to particular people, and reflects their situation. You may interpret 'better received' as meaning that they are more likely to take the action you want.

Information is power

Some reports can be written perfectly well from what you already know; others require **research**.

It is essential to have all the facts that will be necessary to write the report at your fingertips *before* you put anything down on paper. You will do a better job than if you are constantly having to pause and obtain information as you go along. At the very least, this can disrupt your thinking; at worst, your report may be missing vital information.

Sometimes the necessary research is routine: just looking up a file, talking to a colleague or consulting an earlier document. It may be the work of a few moments – a quick telephone call or a word with a colleague on the stairs.

On other occasions the research will be more elaborate. It may mean referring to external as well as internal sources: anything from a business library to the information section of a trade association or chamber of commerce.

Always ask yourself what will help to put you in a position to write a better report; but remember there is a balance to be struck here. Endless research may over-engineer the task and prove unnecessary and time-consuming, while insufficient research may jeopardise the possibility of achieving your objectives. The right amount of research may actually *reduce* subsequent writing time. Certainly it is a mistake to think that skimping research saves time; often the reverse is true.

So, with your objectives clearly in mind, a clear view of your intended reader and your research done – what next? Start to write? Not yet; a systematic approach makes the task easier and that entails factors that still fall under the 'preparation' heading.

A systematic approach

It is not only necessary to 'engage the brain before the pen' (or these days the keyboard), but vital to think through in advance what a report must contain and, for that matter, not contain. The following is recommended solely for its practicality (it is how this book began) and can be adapted to cope with a report of any length or complexity and for any purpose.

There are six stages:

Stage 1. Listing

Forget about sequence, structure and arrangement; just concentrate on and list – in short note (or keyword) form – every significant point that the report might usefully contain. Give yourself plenty of space (a bigger sheet than the standard A4 is often useful: it lets you see everything at one glance). And set down the points as they occur to you, at random across the page.

You will find that this process – akin to 'Mind Mapping®' – is a good thought-prompter. It enables you to fill out the picture as one thought leads to another, the freestyle approach removing the need to pause and try to link points or worry about sequence. With this done (and with some reports it may take only a short time) you can move on to the second stage.

Stage 2. Sorting

Now, you can review what you have noted down and begin to bring some order to it, deciding:

- What comes first, second and so on
- What logically links together, and how
- What provides evidence, example or illustration to the points.

At the same time, you can – and probably will – add some things and have second thoughts about others, which you will delete. You need to bear in mind here what length is indicated, and what will be acceptable.

This stage can often be completed simply by annotating and amending the first stage document. Using a second colour makes this quick and easy, as do link lines, arrows and other enhancements of the original notes.

Stage 3. Arranging

Sometimes, at the end of stage 2, you have a note that is sufficiently clear for you to work from directly. Otherwise, it may be worth rewriting it as a neat list; or this could be the stage at which you put it on screen if you are working that way.

Final revision is possible as you do this. You should be left with a list reflecting the content, emphasis, level of detail and so on that you feel is appropriate. You may well find you are pruning a bit to make things manageable at this stage, rather than searching for more contents and additional points to make.

Stage 4. Reviewing

Sufficient thought may have been brought to bear through earlier stages to render this stage unnecessary. However, for something particularly complex or important (or both) it may be worth running a final check over what you now have written down. Sleep on it first perhaps, and certainly avoid finalising matters straightaway – it is easy to find you have got too close to be objective and cannot see the wood for the trees.

Make any final amendments to the list (if it is on screen this is a simple matter) and use this as your final 'route map' for writing.

Stage 5. Writing

Now you write. Or type or dictate. This is where the real work is, though the earlier preparation will have helped to make it easier and quicker to get the words down.

A couple of tips:

- If possible, *choose the right moment*. There seem to be times when words flow more easily than others. Also, interruptions can disrupt the flow and make writing take much longer, as you recap and restart again and again. Choosing the right time and ensuring that you have uninterrupted time in a comfortable environment both help

- *Keep writing*. Do not pause and agonise over a phrase, a heading or some other detail. You can always come back to that; indeed, it may be easier to complete later. If you keep writing you maintain the flow, allowing consistent thinking to carry you through to the end. Once you have the report down in its entirety you can go back and fine-tune the detail.

Stage 6. Editing

There are three rules about editing: do it, do it and do it. This reminds me of the Somerset Maugham saying, 'There are three rules for writing the novel. Unfortunately no one knows what they are' – but I digress. And I will digress some more, to suggest that there is room in business writing for the occasional aside. It can operate not only as a welcome breather, but also as a memory jogger or a means of adding emphasis.

Where were we? Editing – nothing, but nothing can be sent out without some revision. Few people – if they are honest – can write any significant amount of material so well first time that it requires no amendment at all. So there is no need to feel like a failure if you find you do need to edit. This is another thing that improves with practice. As you write more you will find you do get nearer and nearer to the final product first time and the need to edit and amend reduces.

Reading and checking will also help to catch errors not just of writing, but also of production. The spell-checking feature on most word-processing systems is not perfect, failing for example to recognise names, or transpositions like there/their. Beyond this, of course, editing aims to perfect the text in terms of content and style. As such the following may help the process:

- Leave things a while after writing them; often they look different after a break or a spell doing something else; overnight is good
- Get a colleague to read it. It is often surprising how a fresh look can prompt new thoughts, and thus lead to changes that would otherwise not be made. Pick someone who is willing to be honest, and be prepared to return the favour – it can be time-consuming for them
- Be thorough, worry about the detail. You are not just looking for things that do not make sense, but working to ensure that every detail contributes to the precise impression and emphasis you want to give. Just breaking a long sentence into two, or rephrasing something by a word or two may well make a significant difference. This whole process is important and not to be skimped; this is true of every stage, but perhaps especially of editing.

At the end of the day you need to find a version of the procedures set out in this chapter that works for you. You need to be comfortable with your chosen approach. Provided it remains consciously designed to achieve what is necessary, it will become a habit, and guarantee that you always turn out something which you are confident meets the requirements of the occasion.

All this must be done while keeping in mind the importance of structure, and it is to this that we turn in the next chapter.

3

SHAPE AND STRUCTURE

All the best stories have a beginning, a middle and an end. Reports are no different – they need a clear structure. This is for two reasons: readers will find them easier to follow, and be more likely to read and keep reading; and they will be quicker and easier to create.

Structure demands logic and logic demands clear objectives. The question of *why* the report is being written has already been mentioned; this must remain clearly in mind as consideration is given to, and decisions made about, the structure. Although something more complex than a beginning, a middle and an end may be needed, this makes a good starting point and may, in some cases, be sufficient.

Consider those divisions first:

1. The beginning

On one level the beginning can be taken simply as the introduction. As such its intentions are to:

- Set the scene (which includes linking to relevant past discussions, terms of reference, etc)
- Make clear the topic and the theme
- Set out the objectives and purpose
- Commence the process of getting into the topic, and create a thread that the reader will want to follow through.

  Note. The communication technique of signposting is very useful here. This gives a clear indication of what is coming: 'So, here we will review the staffing, cost, timing and logistics of the project, starting with the staffing implications.' If readers react well to such information, agreeing mentally that what is indicated seems sensible, or just what they wanted or expected, then they are likely to read on more attentively. This is something that is always appreciated and therefore difficult to overuse.
- Position the report as appropriate for the reader (and as something they will want, or recognise they need, to read).

So far, so sensible. But there is a wider view to be taken. Readers bring a set of prejudices to the report. They are asking things like: 'Do I need to read this? Will it be interesting? Readable? Will it help me? Is it important?' A report must *earn* a reading.

The beginning of your report must 'hook' the reader, so make sure that the beginning really does engender the specific reactions you want. Remember, judgements are made very quickly. First impressions last, as the old saying has it, so make sure they are the right ones. Get off to a good start. It helps you and helps the reader. Both of you know where the report is going and why, and both see the advantage in getting to the end.

In addition, the beginning says something about the writer. If the start is good and the first impression is of something useful and well thought through and set out, this will influence the reader's feelings about the writer – 'Seems to know what they are talking about'; 'Obviously did their homework'; 'Describes that clearly and well'. So the tone is important as well as the structure and that, of course, overlaps with the way language is used (this is important throughout and is the subject of the next chapter).

Mention of one particular factor is relevant here: the so called **executive summary**. Some reports lend themselves to a style in which the first item is in fact a summary, perhaps of key findings or recommendations. If this is found appropriate and interests the reader, then they are encouraged to read on.

2. The middle

Here sits the bulk of the content. Its comparative length means this section has the greatest need for internal structure and consistency.

Your intentions here should be to:

- Put over the detail of the report's message
- Maintain and develop the reader's interest
- Ensure clarity and a tone appropriate to the readers
- And, quite possibly, to seek acceptance and counter disagreement.

Sometimes the complexity either of the subject-matter or your intentions, or both, mean that a straightforward three-part structure is insufficient. For example, if your report is setting out an argument it may require a more complex structure. There are doubtless various approaches, but for the sake of brevity and simplicity I suggest that the following covers most requirements: the four parts described can be within the main, middle section (hence their appearance here) or replace the overall structure completely. They can be described thus:

(a) Setting out the *situation*

(b) Describing the *implications*

(c) Reviewing the *possibilities*

(d) Making a *recommendation* (or coming to a conclusion).

Such a progression can overlap with (or even replace) the classic beginning, middle and end arrangement; or it can be accommodated within the middle section to provide a substructure if the middle section might otherwise become confusing.

An example will help to make this concept clearer, and show how an argument can be developed through the four stages to allow a sound case to be made (see box).

Structuring the argument

This example postulates an organisation with certain communication problems. A report making suggestions to correct them might have this broad sequence:

1. **The situation**
   This might refer to both the quantity and importance of written communication around, and outside, the organisation. Also to the fact that writing skills were poor, and no standards were in operation, nor had any training ever been done to develop skills or link them to recognised models that would be acceptable throughout the organisation.

2. **The implications**
   These might range from a loss of productivity (because documents took too long to create and had to constantly be referred back for clarification), to inefficiencies or worse resulting from misunderstood communications. It could also include dilution or damage to the corporate image because of poor documents circulating outside the organisation.

3. **The possibilities**
   Here, as with any argument, there are many possible courses of action, all with their own mix of pros and cons. To continue the example, it might range from limiting report writing to a small core group of people, to eliminating paperwork completely or setting up a training programme and subsequent monitoring system to measure the improvements made.

4. **The recommendation**
   Here the 'best' option needs to be set out. Or, in some reports, a number of options must be reviewed from which others can choose. Recommendations need to be specific: addressing exactly what should be done, by whom and when, alongside such details as cost and logistics.

At all stages generalisations should be avoided. Reports should contain facts, evidence, and sufficient 'chapter and verse' for those in receipt of them to see them as an appropriate basis for decision or action.

If you make sure you have a beginning, a middle and an end, your report should fulfil the old maxim about communications which is usually abbreviated to: 'Tell'em, tell'em and tell'em'. In full, this says: Tell people what you are going to tell them (the introduction), tell them in detail (the body of the report); and then tell them what you have told them (summarise).

What else? Well, a number of factors can help to keep this section on track; these include:

- **A logical structure**: selecting, and making explicit to your readers, a way of organising the content (for example, chronologically)
- **'Signposting' intentions**: knowing broadly what is coming (and why) makes reading easier. This is why many documents need a contents page, but it can also be done within the text: 'We will review the project in terms of three key factors: timing, cost and staffing. First, timing . . .' (perhaps followed by a heading saying TIMING). Signposting is difficult to overdo. The clarity it creates and knowing how what is currently being read fits the overall context, are always appreciated by the reader
- **Using headings** (and sub-headings): this is not only a form of signposting, it also breaks up the text visually and makes it easier to work through a page (contrast the style of a modern business book, such as this, with the kind of dense textbook many of us endured at school)
- **Appropriate language**: is important at every stage (see Chapter 4)
- **Using graphics** (visual graphic devices): this encompasses factors such as bold type, capital letters (that is,

typography), and illustrations, including graphs, tables and charts. All promote clarity and are dealt with in Chapter 5.

Gaining acceptance

This is a discreet aim and can be assisted in a number of ways, for example:

- **Relate to specific groups**: general points and argument may not be so effective as those tailored to a specific group. There is no reason why a report cannot do both, with a mixture of paragraphs or points addressed generally and others starting: 'For those new to the organisation' or '. . . those in the sales department . . .', for example
- **Provide proof**: if you are seeking acceptance, you will need to offer something other than your opinion, especially if you could be seen as having a vested interest. So such things as opinion, research, statistics, and tests from elsewhere strengthen your case. Remember, there is a link between the credibility of the source and the weight it will add to your arguments, so you will need to choose carefully exactly how best to make a point
- **Anticipate objections**: there is no merit in ignoring negative points if you are sure they will occur to readers as the report is read, or they will simply invalidate the good points. They are often better met head on, or indeed signposted: 'Some will be asking how . . .? So in the next three paragraphs I will address exactly that.'

The middle section of a report needs to be explicitly linked to the beginning and the end. It should pick up neatly from points made in the introduction, especially if they have a bearing on the structure (which should be consistent throughout). And it should link equally neatly to the end. This means the thread of content needs to weave its way seamlessly throughout the report and across the divide between the three main segments.

One final point is worth adding before moving on to deal with the end; it is sometimes a nice touch if the text towards the end of the middle section acknowledges the stage that has been reached: 'Lastly, one final point before the summary . . .'

3. The end

This may seem like the easy bit: finish and then just stop. But it can present problems. Some reports seem to avoid the end. The middle runs out of structure. It deteriorates into something that keeps saying 'and another thing'. This can be distracting and annoying.

So, avoid:

- **False endings**: I saw a report not so long ago that had the word 'finally', albeit used in slightly different ways, three times among the final paragraphs
- **Overshooting the structure**: wandering on beyond the last heading yet failing actually to move into the end section. This can add a paragraph or several pages, and consist of unnecessary repetition or irrelevant digression.

So what should you do here? The end should have three specific aims:

1. To reach and present a **conclusion** (this reflects the type of document involved and the nature of the argument that it may present)
2. To pull together and **summarise** the content

3. To end **positively**, on a 'high note' or with a flourish. Or, if that is overstating it somewhat (and many reports are concerned with routine matters rather than exciting ones), at least to end with some power and authority, rather than just tail off.

Summarising is not the easiest thing to do succinctly and effectively. Precisely because of this, it represents a particular opportunity. If it is done well, it impresses. Perversely, this may actually help in getting the report the attention it deserves. Realistically, we know that many people glance at the end of a report before deciding to read it through. If the summary is a good sample of what the report contains, it will encourage readers to read carefully through the whole thing.

A summary develops out of the content most easily if the sequence and structure are sensible, sound and logical. A summary is, after all, the natural conclusion of many cases. However you summarise, it is vital that you keep this part of the report comparatively short. (This does not necessarily mean only a few lines; a long, complex, report will often need more than this by way of summary – the important thing is that the summary is an appropriate length relative to the whole report.) The summary needs to be brief but must encapsulate the essence of the content and conclusions, and this is what makes it difficult to compose without careful consideration.

Be prepared to spend a disproportionate amount of time editing and checking the summary. Certainly, it is a waste to slave at length over a long report, and then allow its effectiveness to be diluted or even destroyed by inattention at this vital stage.

Anything further?

It is worth noting that 'the end' may not always be the end. There may be pages following the summary and conclusions. Appendices, which can be used to take certain discrete areas of detail out of the main core of the content are a prime example. This approach allows such areas to be dealt with more minutely, but the main point is to keep the middle section manageable and stop it from becoming too long and having its key arguments submerged in endless detail.

4

THE POWER OF LANGUAGE

The message is one thing; *how* you say it is quite another. Language makes a difference. It can influence understanding, both for better and worse. Communication derailments are easy enough to recognise. Some are amusing. A friend recently took a reluctant child to hospital. There was nothing serious involved, but the sign that greeted them made the youngster more apprehensive: 'EYE OUT DEPARTMENT'.

Obviously wrong, ill-judged or imprecise language is easy enough to avoid, but language needs to be both subtle and precise. One inappropriate word may dilute impact; a paragraph of gobbledegook may destroy all credibility.

Care and attention to detail with regard to language is always worthwhile. If you write well, people will understand you and be more likely to react as you wish. Exactly how you put things has a direct bearing on how they are received; and that in turn has a direct bearing on how well a report succeeds in its objectives, so language can make a very considerable difference.

An appropriate and effective style

How you write is a matter of taste, style and also habit. Unless you studied English language or literature at college or university you have probably had little formal guidance as to how to write and, in the business environment simply follow the prevailing style. How many people faced with writing their first report, on asking for advice, were simply given an old one and told 'something like that'? Lots, I suspect a case of the blind leading the blind. This, as much as anything, has led to the perpetuation of a rather over-formal, bureaucratic style that does many a report no good.

How you *need* to write must stem in the main from the expectations your intended readers have of what they want to read, or, in some cases, are prepared to read, because – be honest – reading some business documents is always going to be something of a chore; yes, even some of those you write yourself.

What readers expect

Readers want documents to be understandable, readable, straightforward and natural. Each of these is commented on in turn:

Understandable

Clarity has been mentioned already. Its necessity may seem self-evident, though the standard of too many reports suggests the opposite is true. It is all too easy to find everyday examples of wording that is less than clear.

A favourite of mine is a sign you see in some shops: 'EARS PIERCED, WHILE YOU WAIT'. Is there some other way? Maybe there has been a technological development of which I am unaware.

Clarity is assisted by many of the elements mentioned in this chapter, but three factors help immensely:

- Using the right words: for example, are you writing about *recommendations* or *options*, about *objectives* (desired results) or *strategies* (routes to achieving objectives), and when do you use *aims* or *goals*?
- Using the right phrases: what is *24-hour service* exactly (other than insufficiently specific)? Ditto *personal service*? Is this just saying it is done by people? If so, this amounts to stating the obvious; perhaps it needs expanding to explain the nature and advantages of the particular service approach.
- Selecting and arranging words to ensure your meaning is clear: for example, saying 'At this stage, the arrangement is . . .' implies that later it will be something else, when this might not be intended. Saying something is 'about 11.2 per cent' causes confusion. Is it an estimate, as the word 'about' indicates? Or is it as accurate as stating it to a precise decimal point implies? Saying 'After working late into the night, the report will be with you this afternoon' implies that it is the report rather than the writer that was working late.

Readable

Readability is difficult to define, but we all know it when we experience it. Your writing must flow. One point must lead to another, the writing must strike the right tone, inject a little variety and, above all, there must be a logical and explicit structure to carry the message along. As well as the basic shape discussed in the previous chapter, 'signposting' – briefly flagging what is to come – helps in a practical sense by ensuring that the reader understands where something is going. It makes them read on, confident that they are heading in the right direction (this section starts just that way, by listing points to come). It is difficult to overuse signposting and it can be used at several levels within the text.

Straightforward

In a word (or two): simply put. Follow the well-known acronym KISS – **K**eep **I**t **S**imple, **S**tupid. This means using:

- Short words: why 'elucidate' something when you can 'explain'? Similarly, although 'experiment' and 'test' do have slightly different meanings, 'test' may have more impact.
- Short phrases: do not say 'at this moment in time' when you mean 'now', or 'respectfully acknowledge' something when you can simply say 'I thank you'
- Short sentences: too many long sentences is a common fault of business reports. However, short sentences should be mixed in with longer ones, or reading becomes rather like the action of a machine gun. Many sentences are overlong because they mix two rather different points. Break these into two and the overall readability improves
- Short paragraphs: if there are plenty of headings and bullet points it should be difficult to get this wrong, but keep an eye on it. Regular and appropriate breaks as the report progresses do make for easy reading.

Natural

In the same way that some people are said, disparagingly, to have a special 'telephone voice', so some write in an unnatural fashion. Such a style may just be old-fashioned or bureaucratic. However, it can be exacerbated by the writer's self-importance, or by attempts to make a topic seem more weighty than it is. Just a few words can change the tone: saying 'the writer' may easily sound pompous, for instance, especially if there is no reason not to say 'I' (or 'me').

The lesson here is clear and provides a guideline for good writing. Reports need some degree of formality, but always remember that they are an alternative to talking to people. They should be as close to speech as is reasonably possible. I am not suggesting you overdo this, either by becoming too chatty or too relaxed: do not write 'won't' (which you might acceptably say) when 'will not' is genuinely more suitable. However, if you compose what you write much as you would say it and then tighten it up, the result is often better than when you set out to create something which is 'formal business writing'.

All these four factors have a strong influence on writing style, but they do not act alone. Other points are important. Some examples, based very much on what people say they want in what they read, are now dealt with in the following bullet points. Make your writing:

- *Brief*: the gut reaction of readers is to want a document to be brief, but this should not be an end in itself – a better word might be . . .
- *Succinct*: this makes clear that length is inextricably linked to message. If there is a rule, it is to make something long enough to carry the message – then stop

- *Relevant*: this goes with the first two. Not too long, covering what is required, and without irrelevant content or digression.

Note. Comprehensiveness is *never* an objective. If your reports touched on absolutely everything they would certainly be too long. If you do not say everything, then everything you do say is a choice – you need to make good content choices

- *Precise*: say exactly what you mean and get all the details correct. Be careful not to use words or phrases such as: 'about', 'I think', 'maybe' when you should be using something specific
- *In 'our' language*: this is important in many ways. It should be pitched at the right level (of technicality or complexity). It should take account of the readers' past experience and frame of reference (which means you have to know something about what these are). It should 'ring bells with them', indeed it commands more attention and appreciation if it gives the impression of being deliberately tailored to their situation.

Readers' dislikes

Readers hope that what they must read will *not* be:

- *Introspective*: it is appropriate in most business documents to use the word 'you' more than 'I' (or 'we', 'the company', 'the department' etc.). Saying: 'I will circulate more detailed information soon' might be better phrased as 'You will receive more information soon'. Better still, add a phrase like 'so that you can judge for yourselves'. This approach is especially important if you are trying to persuade

- *Patronising*: I once heard a snippet of a schools broadcast on radio with someone saying: 'Never talk down to people, never be condescending. You *do know* what condescending *means,* don't you?' Enough said
- *Biased*: at least where it intends not to be. Managers writing to staff setting out why they think something is a good idea, then asking for their staff's views, may elicit more agreement than is actually felt. If views are sought, it is better simply to set something out and ask for comment without expressing a positive personal view in advance
- *Politically incorrect*: there is considerable sensitivity about this that should neither be ignored nor underestimated. For example, as there is still no word that means 'he or she', some contrivance may be necessary in this respect. Similarly, choice of words needs care. I was pulled up the other day for using the expression 'manning the office'. As I was referring to who was on duty at what times, rather than anything to do with recruitment or selection (which the suggested alternative of 'staffing' seemed to me to imply), this seemed somewhat absurd at the time. But if it matters to someone, it matters, and while you should not allow your writing to become awkward or contrived to accommodate such considerations, some care is certainly necessary.

There is a considerable amount to bear in mind here. The focus must be on the reader throughout. However, you must not forget your own position as the writer; there are certain things that must be incorporated into your writing.

The writer's approach

Every organisation has an image: this is not in question. What is open to debate is whether this just happens, for good or ill, or if it is seen as something to actively create, maintain and make positive. Similarly, every report or proposal you write says something about you. Whether you like it or not this is true. And it matters. The profile, whether wittingly or unwittingly presented, may influence whether people believe, trust or like you. It may influence how they feel about your expertise, or whether they can see themselves agreeing with you or doing business with you.

Your personal profile also has the potential to affect your career. It is unavoidable that, given the prominent role played by paperwork in most organisations, what you write typecasts you in the eyes of others – including your boss – as the sort of person who is going places, or not.

Your prevailing style, and what a particular document says about you, is well worth thinking about. You cannot afford to let the opportunity presented slip by, you need to consciously influence it. Start by considering what you want people to think of you. Take a simple point. You want to be thought of as efficient. The style of the document surely says something about this. If it is good, contains everything the reader wants, and covers everything it said it would, then the reader will gain an impression of efficiency.

There is a plethora of characteristics that you might want your writing to reflect. Ask yourself exactly how you want various factors to come over. For example:

- What knowledge (of the subject, the people, the situation) should be evident?
- How can your empathy with people (immediate readers or others), and/or interest in them be shown?

- What level of expertise should be reflected?
- How is your confidence demonstrated (or enhanced)?
- Does what you say have sufficient 'clout'?
- Is your case put over with honesty and sincerity?
- Do you sound reliable?
- Is your decisiveness evident?

All the above, and more, can help you ascertain exactly how to achieve the effect you want. It may also be important to appear well organised, concerned with detail, or to position yourself in a particular role: as adviser, say, or honest broker. Such images are cumulative. They build up over time and can assist in the establishment and maintenance of relationships, whether with a colleague, a customer, or the boss.

Similarly, you might have in mind a list of characteristics you want actively to avoid seeming to embrace. For example, appearing dogmatic, patronising, inflexible or old-fashioned in your job might do you little good. Other characteristics are sometimes to be emphasised, sometimes not. Stubbornness is a good example.

Such images are not created in a word. There is more to appearing honest than writing: 'Let me be completely honest . . .' (which might actually have the effect of making alarm bells ring!). Your intended profile will arise, in part, from specifics such as choice of words, but also from the whole way in which you use language. So we now move on to a more detailed examination of the use of language.

The use of language

How language is used makes a difference to exactly how a message is received. The importance of using the right word has already been touched on, and the kind of difference we are talking about can be well demonstrated by changing no more than one word. For example, consider the first sentence of this paragraph: 'How language is used makes a difference to exactly how a message is received'. Try adding one word '. . . makes a big difference to . . .'

Now let us see what happens if we change that word 'big'. It is surely a little different to say '. . . makes a great difference . . .' and there are many alternatives 'real', 'powerful', 'considerable', 'vast', 'special', 'large', 'important'. You can doubtless think of more. In the context of what I am actually saying here, powerful is a good word. It is not just a question of how you use language, but what you achieve by your use of it.

Note. No report writer should be without both a dictionary and thesaurus beside their desk; the latter is often the most useful. Even a simple word like 'useful' can be substituted by advantageous, beneficial, convenient, effective, fruitful, helpful, practical, salutary, valuable – the list goes on. Your choice of vocabulary influences precision of expression. Grammar and punctuation have a vital role to play too (though it is beyond the scope of this book to review either in detail).

Making language work for you

I regularly see examples of business writing that are almost wholly devoid of adjectives. Yet surely one of the first purposes of language is to be **descriptive**. Most writing necessitates the painting of a picture to some degree at least. Contrast two phrases:

'Smooth as silk'

'Sort of shiny'

The first (used, now I think of it, as a slogan by Thai Airways) conjures up a clear and precise picture. The second phrase could mean almost anything; dead wet fish are sort of shiny, but they are hardly to be compared with the touch of silk.

Expectations of complexity (and cognitive cost) were mentioned earlier, and to some extent it does not matter whether something is short or long: whatever it is, if it makes things effortlessly clear, it is appreciated. And if it is descriptive at the same time as it makes something easier to understand, then readers will be doubly appreciative.

Clear description may need working at, but the effort is worthwhile. I recently wrote asking a meeting venue to set up for a seminar arranging a group 'in a U-shape'. When I arrived the arrangement certainly put people in a U, but did so around a boardroom-style table. But I meant a U in the sense of an open U, one that gave me the ability to stand within the U and work with delegates. If I had said that, there could have been no misunderstanding.

Description is important, but sometimes we want more than that. We want something to be descriptive, but also **memorable**. It seems to me that this is achieved in two ways: first by something that is descriptive yet unusual; second, when it is descriptive and unexpected.

Returning to the venue theme above, I once heard a conference executive describe, in the course of an explanation about room layouts, a U shape as 'putting everyone in the front row'. That, I believe, is descriptive and memorable because, while clear, it is also an unusual way of expressing the idea. Such phrases have considerable impact and are worth searching for.

To demonstrate the second approach to being memorable, I will use a description I put in a report. In summarising a perception survey (researching customers' and contacts' views of a client organisation) I wanted to describe how the majority of people reported. They liked them and were well disposed towards using them, but also found them a little bureaucratic, slow and less efficient and innovative than they would ideally like. I wrote that they were seen as 'being like a favourite, and comfortable old sofa, when people wanted them to be like a modern, leather executive chair'. Clearly, this is descriptive, but it gained not just from being unusual, but by being unexpected in a business writing context. I know it was memorable, because it was used at subsequent meetings by the organisation's own people to describe the changes that the report had highlighted as necessary.

As well as being memorable, this kind of approach works well to convey something of the writer's personality.

Another element you may want, on occasion, to put into your writing is **emotion**. If you want to seem enthusiastic, interested, surprised or whatever, let it show. A dead, passive style (. . . 'the results were not quite as expected, they showed that' . . .) is not the same as one that characterises what is said with emotion – '. . . you will be surprised by the results, which showed that . . .' Both may be appropriate on occasion, but the latter is often neglected when in fact it could add considerably to the impact of the report.

Consider this. How often when you are searching for the right phrase do you reject something as either insufficiently formal or conventional? Be honest. Too often people are on the brink of putting down something that will be memorable or which will add power, and then they play safe and opt for something else. It may be adequate, but it fails to impress; it is a lost opportunity.

Next, we look at some common pitfalls.

Mistakes to avoid

Some elements may act to dilute the power of your writing. They may or may not be technically wrong, but they end up reducing your effectiveness and making your objectives less certain to be achieved. For example:

Blandness

Watch out! This is a regular trap for the business writer. It happens not so much because you make the wrong choice, as because you are writing on automatic pilot without thought, or at least sufficient thought, or attention to detail.

What does it mean to say something is:

- *Quite* good (or bad)
- *Rather* expensive?

What exactly is:

- An *attractive* promotion? (as opposed to a profit-generating one, perhaps)
- A *slight* delay? (For a moment or a month?)

All these give only a vague impression. Ask yourself exactly what you want to express, then choose language that does just that.

'Officespeak'

This is another all too common component of some business writing. It may confuse little, but it adds little, other than an old-fashioned feel. Here are a few examples:

- Enclosed 'for your perusal' or enclosed 'for your interest'. (You may need to tell them why it should be of interest; or 'enclosed' alone may suffice)
- 'We respectfully acknowledge receipt of . . .' (why not say 'Thank you'?)

- 'In the event that' ('if' is surely better)
- 'Very high speed operation' (fast)
- 'Conceptualised' (thought)

Avoid such trite approaches like the plague, and work to rid yourself of any 'pet' phrases you use habitually, too often and inappropriately.

Faddy language

New words and phrases enter the language almost daily, while others fall into disuse. It is worth watching for the life cycle of such words because, if you are out of step, they may fail to do the job you want. I notice three stages:

1. When it is too early to use them: they will either not be understood, or seem silly – a failed attempt at trendiness
2. When they work well
3. When their use begins to date and they sound incongruous or inadequate.

Examples may date too, but let me try. I twitched visibly when someone on BBC Radio 4 referred to an 'upcoming' event. For me at least, this is at stage 1. and does not sound right at all; 'forthcoming' will suit me well for a while longer.

On the other hand, what did we say before we said 'mission statement'? This is certainly a term in current use. Most people in business appreciate its meaning and many make good use of it.

What about a word or phrase that is past its best? I suggest a common one: 'user friendly'. At first it was new, nicely descriptive and quickly began to be useful. Now, I suspect, with no single gadget on the entire planet not so described by its makers, it is becoming hackneyed.

Mistakes people hate

A simple example is the word 'unique', which is so often used with an adjective. Unique means like nothing else. Nothing can be 'very unique' or 'greatly unique'. Think of similar examples which annoy you and avoid them too. How about:

- 'Different to' (different from)
- 'Less' (relates to quantity but is often used erroneously when number is involved, and 'fewer' would be correct
- Unnecessary inverted commas (which are becoming a modern 'plague').

Clichés

This is a difficult one. Any overused phrase can become categorised as a cliche. Yet a phrase like 'putting the cart before the horse' is not only well known, but establishes an instant and precise vision and can therefore be useful. People like to conjure up a familiar image and so such phrases should not always be avoided. Also, reports may not be the place for creative alternatives like 'spread the butter before the jam'.

Following the rules

What about **grammar**, **syntax** and **punctuation**? Of course they matter – but, remember, some of the rules were made to be broken and some of the old rules are no longer regarded as rules, certainly not for business writing.

Certain things can jar. For example:

- Poor punctuation: too little is exhausting to read, especially coupled with long sentences. Too much seems affected and awkward. Certain rules do matter here, but the simplest guide is probably breathing. We learn to punctuate speech long before we write anything, so in writing all that is really necessary is a conscious inclusion of the pauses. The length of pause and the nature of what is being said indicate the most appropriate solution

- Tautology (unnecessary repetition where the meaning has already been conveyed). The classic example is people who say 'I, myself personally'. Do not 'export overseas', simply export; do not indulge in 'forward planning', simply plan
- Oxymorons (two-word paradoxes) may sound silly – 'distinctly foggy' – or provide a vivid way of expressing something – 'deafening silence'. Some sentences can cause similar problems of contradiction: 'I never make predictions; and I never will'.

Some rules are still regarded as sacrosanct by purists, but breaking them can work well in business writing and, indeed, is often commonplace. A good example here is the rule that you should never begin a sentence with the words 'and' or 'but'. But you can. And it helps to produce tighter writing and avoid overlong sentences. But, or rather however, it also makes another point; do not overuse this sort of device.

Another similar rule is that sentences should not end with prepositions. 'He is a person worth talking to' really does sound easier on the ear than '. . . with whom it is worth talking'. Winston Churchill is said to have responded to criticism about this with the famous line: 'This is a type of arrant pedantry up with which I will not put.'

Still other rules may be broken only occasionally. Many of us have been brought up never to split infinitives, and it often causes annoyance. There are exceptions, however.

Would the most famous one in the world, from *Star Trek*, 'To boldly go where no man has gone before' really be better as '. . . to go boldly . . .?' I do not think so.

Don't forget that spelling matters too – although these days spellcheckers can compensate for any inadequacies in that area.

Note. If you want a guide to the real detail here, from when to use a colon and when to use a semicolon, then let me recommend some further reading. There are a plethora of 'good English' guides, many of them reference books: something like Bloomsbury's *Good Word Guide* is certainly useful. Head and shoulders above the rest, however (if that is not a cliché) and something many will really enjoy reading is *English Our English*. Written by Keith Waterhouse, the novelist and newspaper columnist, and published by Penguin, it is a comprehensive guide, but it is interesting, often funny and projects a great enthusiasm for writing. Buy one at once.

Style

Finally, most people have, or develop, a way of writing that includes things they simply like. Why not indeed? For example, although the rule books now say they are simply alternatives, I think that to say: 'First, . . ., secondly, . . . and thirdly, . . .', has much more elegance than beginning: 'Firstly, . . .'. I am not sure why.

It would be a duller world if we all did everything the same way and writing is no exception. There is no harm in using some things for no better reason than that you like them. It is likely to add variety to your writing and make it seem distinctive, which may be useful in itself.

Certainly, you should always be happy that what you write *sounds* right. To quote Keith Waterhouse: 'If, after all this advice, a sentence still reads awkwardly, then what you have there is an awkward sentence. Demolish it and start again.'

However carefully you strive to write clearly and in a way that creates an impact, the effect will be spoilt if the report appears less than professional. The final element that helps to create the sort of report that will do the job you want is making sure it looks right. So it is on this that we will spend a few pages before pulling our 30-minute review together.

5

THE RIGHT LOOK

Even with modest skills and with equipment that is less than state of the art, it is possible for someone to produce documentation that looks very professional. Prevailing standards are, for the most part, good and, as the capabilities of laser printers, computers and associated equipment advance, standards improve too.

Of course, it is possible to overdo things. Too much colour, too many graphs, or a profusion of typefaces and sizes may be distracting. The purpose of good presentation is to influence the reception a report receives favourably, by making it more likely to be read, easier to read and thus that much more likely to achieve its chosen purpose.

So what exactly does enhance clarity, produce appropriate emphasis and project the right image? There is, of course, no one magic formula or indeed any one standard layout we should all adopt. A plethora of factors is important, and this chapter reviews the range of options from which combinations may be selected and approaches which then combine to create the look you want.

There are four main areas to consider here:

- The format and elements (and how they are arranged)
- The layout of the pages
- The use of exhibits (graphs, charts, etc)
- The overall 'packaging' of the report itself

which are reviewed here in turn.

The format of a report

The right format depends on a number of factors: the length of the report, its complexity, the nature of the recipients and even the prevailing style and culture of an organisation. It is important to find the right balance. Make something too formal and it may be seen as using a sledgehammer to crack a nut, and thus time-wasting for all concerned. Make it too informal and it may be seen as not doing its topic justice and treating an important issue too lightly.

So, consider whether you need, and if so how you will use, the following:

- *A title page*: all reports need a clear title and some will need this on a dedicated front page; this may also include the date, a reference, the writer's name, even a circulation list (though there is merit in keeping this page largely uncluttered)
- *A contents page*: it is not usually difficult to decide if length or complexity make this necessary. It is important that readers can find their way around a report, both as they read it and when they are discussing – 'Let's all turn to the section on Timing on page 14' – so the detail here can vary from brief headings to a more detailed description of what different sections cover.

- *An index*: only the most complex report will need an index at the end as well as a contents page. But some documents warrant it and it should be carefully compiled and lead easily to whatever readers might want
- *Appendices*: these act to separate details from the main argument or flow of a report, thus keeping the main part manageable: for example, keeping detailed costings separate and positioning them at the end of the report.

An appendix is a very useful device, though the details positioned in this way must be as well presented as anything included in the body of the report. In technical reports it effectively allows two levels of technicality to be pursued together: one reader may elect to go through the appendices in detail, while another will be content with an overview and will only scan the detail.

Appendices are usually placed at the end of a report, so the main text must always refer exactly to what is available in an appendix, saying how it relates to the main content and giving a clear page reference to allow readers to digress or fill in detail if they wish.

Sometimes appendices may consist of material imported into the report and thus presented in a different style. It is possible to bind in elements such as technical literature, a press release or whatever, though their style and presentation must not dilute the standard of the report as a whole.

The layout of the pages

Again, there are numbers of factors which can be deployed, or not, to create the overall look desired:

- *Space*: dense text can be off-putting and difficult to read. Furthermore, if you consider how a report is used –

annotated with notes, passed round, discussed at meetings and so on – then allowing sufficient space for this to happen conveniently is appreciated by readers. So, do not cramp the margins, allow sufficient space between paragraphs or sections, select type spacing (double spaced, one and a half?) carefully and balance length in terms of pages with an overall layout that looks, and indeed is, easy to use

- *Page layout*: with the ability of most word-processing systems to summon up a range of devices at the touch of a button, some sensible decisions are needed here. For example, should headings be extra large, indented or centred? The options here are legion. Remember, it is what suits the reader that matters most; resist the temptation to tinker or embellish just for fun
- *Typeface and size*: do not mix too many typefaces together, and pick a style that is readable. You may need to link to standard practice and company policy here, for example to match well with the organisation's letterhead and reflect a corporate image. You may also need to adapt to achieve particular things, for example using a small typeface to set aside a footnote at the end of a page
- *Emphasis*: one of the most important things to bear in mind is how layout contributes to your intended emphasis. This may be as simple as putting just one word in *italics* to highlight meaning. You can also select to use:

  — CAPITAL LETTERS

  — **bold type** (or **BOTH**)

  — underlining

  — indenting

— bullet points in one of their many designs

— or boxed paragraphs

Such devices may be combined: a paragraph in an indented box, set in italics, say, though be careful of overdoing things or you will succeed only in distracting or annoying. One clear device such as **the use of bold type** to highlight something within a sentence or paragraph stands out and adds emphasis.

- *Page breaks*: a new page makes a real break and thus gives emphasis to whatever heading you start with over the page. Again conscious thought and decision are necessary here and there are alternatives – for example, you may arrange something deliberately so that the reader must turn over a page in the middle of a sentence to increase the chances of their reading on
- *Numbering*: numbers provide an invaluable guide to finding your way around a report. Pages should always be numbered. In addition, you need a clear system for numbering headings and sub-headings. If there are several levels of heading you can make this clear also, thus:

— **1. Main heading**

— *i) Sub-heading*

and so on, varying numbering (or using letters: A or a), for example) and linking to a suitable type style as appropriate. In addition, you can number paragraphs (though this always looks very formal and is therefore not a good choice for everything) using **1, 1.1, 1.2, 1.3**, etc (the main heading is numbered **1**, then subsequent subparagraphs are numbered **1.1**, etc) which allows very precise references to be made and can be used to locate position very accurately in discussion. The level of overall complexity must be your guide here.

The use of exhibits

The old saying that a picture is worth a thousand words is not without truth. Some things are best explained using a series of visual devices that stand out from the text and which I am referring to here as exhibits.

A series of examples, shown opposite, summarises the key possibilities that are available to create this effect.

Simplicity is vital here. Two simple charts may act to make things clearer than a single more complex one – and be easier and quicker to prepare. Bear in mind what the reader *really needs* rather than looking only at what a system makes possible. You do not want to waste time creating a complex chart which readers see as only of peripheral interest and do no more than glance at.

Equally, modern technology may allow you to usefully include all sorts of things – full colour pictures, say – and everything has its place; though not all at once and not every time.

The overall 'packaging' of a report

The humble paperclip has its uses, but reports demand something better. Most need some form of binding.

Again, there are options. A short, perhaps transient document, circulated only internally may need no more than a staple at the corner. Otherwise, a variety of binding systems can be used. Many favour, for good reason, those that allow turned pages to lie flat. Sometimes it is appropriate to have a printed cover; sometimes a sheet of transparent plastic which allows the title page to speak for itself is more suitable.

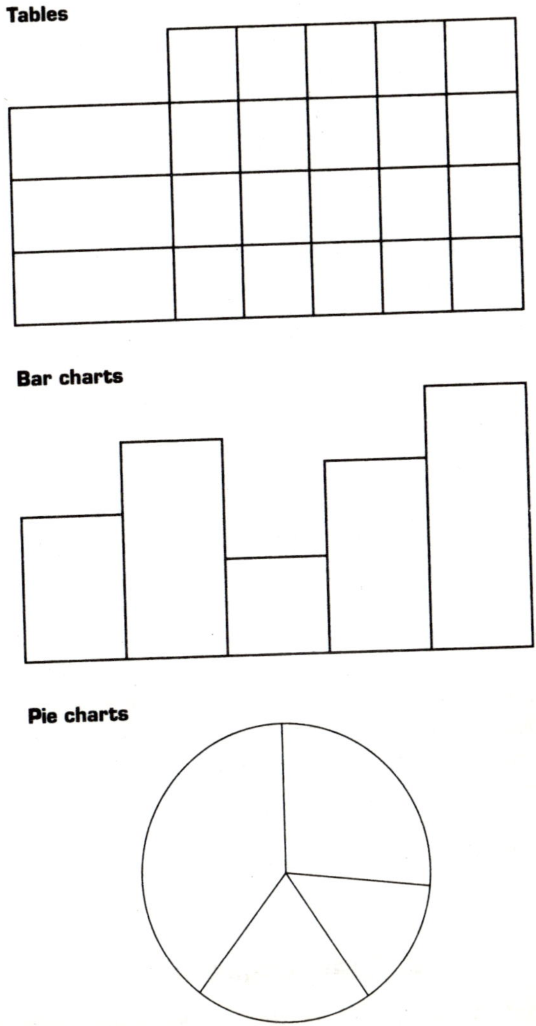

Figure 5.1 Examples of tables and charts

There are a number of ways binding can boost the overall look of the report. For example:

- the colour of the report cover can match a letterhead
- a report cover with a flap to allow smaller brochures or pieces of print to accompany the report
- the facility to attach a business card.

Decisions here must combine matters of taste with more practical considerations and, as with everything else, the final arbiter is the reader and your view of what will suit them.

Cost is always a consideration and different methods incur different costs. But it is a pity to spoil the ship for a ha-p'orth of tar, and a report may be so important that minor cost differences are irrelevant. Again, a balance should be struck: for example, with a long report which is going to be widely circulated, it may make sense to go for quality binding, but print the document itself on both sides of the paper, thus reducing bulk and making a small cost saving.

Finally, think about the method of despatch, particularly externally. Things need to be on time and couriers have their place, but however a document is sent, it is worth thinking of how it will arrive at the other end – a strong or padded envelope may be needed to ensure that something arrives looking as smart as when it went out.

Technology can be – is – wonderful, but may lessen impact. For example, E-mail is undeniably fast, but removes your ability to package something as an impressive document.

A final judgement

At the end of the day the readers decide what looks right. If they think a report is suitably presented and find its format practical, all will be well (provided they like what they read – packaging can never make up for inadequate content!).

If the layout is appropriate to the purpose, the content is well signposted and the report easy to find your way around, things are illustrated as necessary and the intended emphasis shines through, then the packaging will be playing its part.

As has been said stated throughout, there may well be a great deal hanging on a report's reception. None of the factors that help to strengthen the impact are to be sneezed at, and if attention to detail in all matters of presentation can increase impact even a little, then that attention is well worthwhile.

AFTERWORD

'The trouble with opportunities is that they so often come disguised – as hard work'

Anon

The very title of this book precludes an overelaborate summary. The few words that follow, however, act as a checklist and reminder for future action:

- **Remember the dangers**. Sloppy business writing abounds, and nowhere is it more evident than in reports. The problem is often compounded by the fact that many people regard the task of writing a report as a chore and, concentrating primarily on getting it out of the way, give it less attention than it deserves. Even minor errors – as little as one ill-chosen word – can lead to failure to get a message across
- **Remember the opportunity**. To repeat a phrase applied to reports early on in the book, reports can be the business equivalent of an open goal. Good ones inform, stimulate action, achieve their purposes and can

enhance their writer's reputation in the process. Small variations can make all the difference, with even one well-chosen phrase acting like a lighthouse to guide readers in the right direction

- **Remember the rules**. Few reports succeed without being well prepared, thought through and carefully drafted. A systematic approach, practice, and good habits speed the process and a good report should take no longer to write than a poor and less well considered one; indeed the right approach can speed up the whole writing process. In addition, the structure, sequence and logic must be sensible and the language clear and well chosen for the job it is to do, and the readers for whom it is intended. A clear focus throughout the process on the readers' needs and expectations will also ensure that the final text does the best possible job for you
- **Remember that rules are not always sacrosanct**. Of course, there are some rules it is always wise to observe, but others need flexible application, especially with regard to language. There is no reason for business writing to be so formal that it becomes dull. If it is, it will be less effective at expressing your chosen message; sometimes things do not just need to be clear, they need to be unexpected or memorable as well
- **Remember the purpose**. For your writing to be successful, you must always have clear objectives. Often these reflect the impact you want to have on people – if you intend to persuade people to adopt a point of view, change their opinions or take action, the report must be tailored throughout to achieving just that. Always remember too that reports say something about you; the only choice you have is exactly what that should be.

- **Remember that you can write good reports**. What we have been reviewing here is a skill, and one that can be learned and fine-tuned continuously (as indeed dynamic business circumstances may demand). If you now intend to abandon a few old habits it may take a while, and it will certainly take some conscious effort. But everyone *can* improve their writing style. A little bit of hard work, coupled with a willingness to take heed of criticism, to achieve what you want in this area is eminently worthwhile.

Your reports will be quicker and easier to put together, and they will be more likely to guarantee results.